AGING FAITHFULLY

28 Days of Prayer

Missy Buchanan

UPPER
ROOM BOOKS®
NASHVILLE

The Upper Room Books website: books.upperroom.org

UPPER ROOM®, UPPER ROOM BOOKS®, and design logos are trade-
marks owned by The Upper Room®, a ministry of Discipleship Ministries,®
Nashville, Tennessee. All rights reserved.

Scripture quotations are from **New Revised Standard Version Bible**, ©
copyright 1989 National Council of the Churches of Christ in the United
States of America. Used by permission. All rights reserved.

Cover image: © Willie B. Thomas/Istockphoto.com http://istockphoto.com
Cover design: Left Coast Design, Portland, OR/www.lcoast.com

Library of Congress Cataloging-in-Publication Data
Buchanan, Missy.
  Aging faithfully : 28 days of prayer / Missy Buchanan.
    p. cm.
  ISBN 978-0-8358-1063-0
  1. Older people—Prayers and devotions. 2. Aging—Religious
aspects—Christianity. I. Title.
  BV4580.B77 2011
  242'.65—dc22   2011011193

CONTENTS

INTRODUCTION

You have heard it said that the only time people get excited about being old is when they are young. There is some truth to that. Many people refuse to talk about aging as if they can somehow prevent it from happening. They want to believe that they will never have to face the harsh realities that sometimes accompany a long life.

How easily we forget that God designed aging! Think about it. God is God. God could have created bodies that never changed beyond young adulthood while we continued to age in years. But that is not God's way. Once you truly acknowledge that aging is part of God's plan, you can begin to embrace it as a divine gift.

Each stage of aging offers rich treasures if you choose to mine them. The eyes make all the difference. If your eyes are fixed on the negative images of growing old, you will likely miss the precious nuggets right before you. Fix your eyes on God and you will discover an abiding joy that only comes with a long life.

HOW TO USE THIS BOOK

This book is divided into four weeks, each with a particular theme about aging. Each day's reading supports the week's focus with a scripture, a meditation, and a prayer. It concludes with a suggestion for deeper thought or practical application.

Sunday is the time to gratefully celebrate the culmination of the week's readings. The questions at the end of the book are intended for small-group discussion or as another opportunity for individuals to explore the topics more fully.

Take your time in reading and responding. Let each day's readings wash over you. Prepare your heart to discover what it is to age joyfully.

WEEK 1

Accepting the Challenges of Aging

MONDAY
Out of step

Read Psalm 56:3-4.

A woman pulls her chair up close to a computer and peers into the screen. She sees the image of her grandson, an officer in the military, talking to her as though he is sitting across her dining room table instead of in a war zone halfway around the world. Tears suddenly well up.

In another city a grandfather watches restless grandchildren push buttons on their slim, palm-sized electronic gadgets. One child listens to music on a tiny device with thousands of songs at his fingertips. Two send silent messages to friends in other towns, while the youngest searches a handheld apparatus for show times at a movie theater. The older man shrugs his shoulders in bewilderment.

It is not surprising that both these grandparents feel sharp pangs of insecurity. They used to feel smart and savvy. Not anymore. Not with all this fast-changing technology. As much as they marvel at the wonder of it all, they fear becoming hopelessly out of step with the rest of the world.

You may feel the same. No one likes feeling incompetent—not Moses with his speech impediment, not Abraham who thought he was too old to carry out God's purpose. God chose these men anyway and equipped them for tasks they felt they could not do.

Don't be afraid to learn new skills and acquire new information. Trust God and embrace new opportunities with a willing heart. Always remember, though, priceless qualities like love, faith, integrity, humility, and compassion will never go out-of-date.

Prayer

Gracious God, sometimes I feel like an old-timer stuck in a bygone era. I confess I am afraid of . . .

- *Technology that I don't understand*
- *being alone*
- *increasing health problems*
- *some one breaking into our house*

Grant me courage to trust you and to keep leaning forward in life. Amen.

Suggestion

Select a task or a piece of technology that intimidates you, something you have been afraid to learn. Ask a family member or friend to teach you more about it. Celebrate your effort to learn. At the same time, make note of those timeless, Christlike qualities you hope to exemplify. Make a list of ten of those qualities and post it in your room. Review the list each day this week.

TUESDAY
Losing interest in life

Read Psalm 42:5.

The older man had loved sports for as long as he could remember. He often wondered how many games he had played and watched over the span of his long life. Lately, though, his enthusiasm for sporting events had begun to dwindle. Instead of cheering his favorite team, he often stared mindlessly at a blank television screen. Silently he wondered what happened to his passion for sports. Even more unsettling, he began to think of growing old as some sort of punishment.

Maybe you also have found your mood spiraling down as you have aged. You shudder at the thought of losing your vitality and independence. Activities and pursuits you used to enjoy now seem mundane, even lackluster. You are not the first to feel this way. If your outlook on life has worsened as you have aged, consider the blessings you would have missed if you had not lived a long life. Then give thanks to God.

Old age is not a punishment but a divine gift. Your life experiences have enriched you beyond measure. Your life brims with countless memories, relationships, stories, and images. Now is not the time to unplug from life. Invite a new passion to settle into your thoughts. God can restore a brighter outlook as you look forward to a new day.

Prayer

Heavenly Father, take away the dimness of my soul. I confess that I have allowed ...

myself to stagnate & not reach out to others

to steal my enthusiasm for living. Ignite a passion within me. Reawaken me to your presence. Where there is grayness, let me see color. Enable me to find purpose in living where there seems to be none. Amen.

Suggestion

Be intentional in your effort to rekindle your passion for living. Begin the new day by noticing all the colors outside your window. Be mindful of the many shades and hues. Ponder God's creation. Read a book about a subject you have never before explored. Play a new board game with a grandchild or friend. Ask a neighbor to tell you a story about her childhood.

WEDNESDAY
Same inside

Read Ecclesiastes 3:11-12.

A woman looks into a full-length mirror and sees a stranger. How odd that her outside appearance does not match her inside feelings. She studies her face, how it sags. She looks at her wrinkled hands speckled with age spots. But somehow she feels much the same inside as she did at age twenty.

She still loves big band music, historic lighthouses, and strawberry shortcake, just as she did when she was much younger. It is only when she sees her reflection or feels the pain of arthritis that she remembers she is growing old.

Aging is a curious phenomenon. How do you know when you are old? There is no definitive line in the sand. You don't cross a boundary one day and—poof!—you are suddenly old. No, aging happens gradually, a process that begins at birth and lasts a lifetime. Somewhere along the journey, you begin to notice that your eyes struggle to read the small print. Your knees stiffen when you sit too long. But even as another milestone birthday goes by, you feel the same on the inside.

One fact is certain. If you put your trust in your physical body, eventually you will be betrayed. Though antiaging products and procedures may slow the aging process or at least its evidence, they cannot save you from physical decline. That is why you need to anchor your life in something that won't deteriorate over time. That is why you so desperately need God.

Prayer

Ever-loving God, I am grateful that even though my body has changed over time, you will never change. I thank you for creating me as a person with unique gifts and desires like . . .

Help me to care for my body appropriately but to *Do!* resist putting my faith in flesh and bones. Teach me to trust you as I age, for you are Creator of my ageless soul. Amen. *Health — AIC to higher than 7 ut — 161-164*

Suggestion *Steps — 1500 + each day Sat 9-24 SAT 10-15 9-22 171.2 9-23 171 170.6 169.8*

still nervous walking

In what ways do you feel like you did when you were younger? What still delights you even though your physical body has changed? If you love to travel but can't take long trips, immerse yourself in travel books. *or short trips* Surf the Internet; watch travel shows on TV. Find ways to enjoy the interests and pursuits you always loved. Adapt the method when necessary. Rejoice in all that makes you unique. *Salvage DAWGs — re-use instead of new stuff*

Mon 10-13

Going to grocery & away putting them is hard to do

THURSDAY
Weary arms

Read Isaiah 40:30-31.

Your arms are getting tired. After decades of toting groceries and the week's garbage, now there are days when it's all you can do to summon the energy to open a jug of milk. Sometimes your hands tremble as if they have a mind of their own. You make yourself exercise each morning, honoring the biblical mandate to care for your body. Though exercise undoubtedly is beneficial, you realize your physical strength will never be what it once was.

Over the course of your long life, you have sometimes felt it was up to you to carry the burdens of the world. You struggled to push through pressured days on your own power. At those moments you forgot just how much you needed God. Now you admit you are tired of trying to be strong.

The truth is, God never tires. God's arms are always extended to you. God will never grow weary of lifting you up and carrying you through hard times.

Though your body grows weaker as more years pass, your faith can grow stronger. It is a truth contrary to the ways of the world. Real strength comes when you confess your weakness and lean on God.

Monday 10-3

Prayer

Almighty God, forgive me for trying to be strong on my own. I used to think that it was up to me to carry the weight of . . . *keeping everyone happy, volunteering, pleasing people with food I cooked & baked*

Please increase my faith as I lean on your strength. Encourage me to avoid a sedentary lifestyle as I am able. Today I will exercise and move forward with your help. Amen.

Suggestion

Do this ↓

If you are not already exercising, begin today by walking and doing some strength-building exercises. Just squeezing a ball builds arm and hand muscles. Don't neglect to exercise your spiritual muscles too. Memorize Isaiah 40:31. *Read*

FRIDAY
Loss

Mon 10-3

Read John 16:20.

You have cried many tears in your life. You have let silent waves of sorrow swell in your heart for a loss that can be grieved but never changed. At times the pain was so severe, you would have welcomed death if only it would have come.

No one gets to the far side of life without experiencing profound loss. Family members and friends die. Health crises come. Unwanted change arrives unannounced. At times it seems that too much has been unfairly snatched from your life.

God understands. God has felt the warm tears when you have mourned, has been moved by what moved you. God understands the emotional and physical exhaustion that comes with loss.

God doesn't turn away from your sorrow. God knows the grief of leaving a home where you created memories. God shares the pain of watching your independence slip away. God understands the sadness in watching friends move away and wondering if you will ever see them again.

With every change there is loss. Yet with every loss there is a new beginning. God promises that joy will come in the morning. God celebrates your resiliency, a tenacity that is honed in relationship with your Creator.

Prayer

Almighty God, it is true that I have experienced great loss in my life. I have grieved . . .

about what cant be fixed or forgotten

Thank you for inviting me to pour out my grief before you and for loving me through the darkest days. Give me a gentle acceptance of my circumstances and help me to press on. Amen.

Suggestion

Aging brings change. Some events, like the death of a loved one, cannot be undone. But your attitude and how you choose to live out your days can be changed. Write down ways that you can make positive change in your life. Maybe you could improve your diet or engage in more mental activity. Perhaps you could increase your prayer time. Then ask for God's help to carry out these changes. Check your list regularly and hold yourself accountable.

— Track my food & activity, Lose 10 lbs I lost nov. Dec 2021
— Read Bible
— De Clutter House
*   " Closet*
—

SATURDAY
Invisible

Read Isaiah 49:15-16.

A slightly stooped man walks into the room. Not so long ago, his frame would have filled the doorway. Now it seems that no one can see him at all. He feels invisible to the rest of the world. Edging close to a chair, he lets his body drop into the soft cushions. Another day has gone by without a phone call or a visit. He closes his eyes and steels himself for one more round of disappointment.

When you think people are too busy with their lives to remember you, you get an awful feeling. As you have aged, you may have felt unimportant or overlooked at times. In fact, it may seem that you too have lost much of your identity. You don't want others' pity. You don't want to be treated like a child. You just wish that people could see you as the real person you are, with feelings and a long past.

Never forget one thing: you matter greatly to God. You are not worthless. You are not a castaway. Remember what God has already done for you in years past. Be confident that God still has a mission for you.

Accept the fact that you cannot change others. Pray for them; don't try to manipulate them. Instead, focus on being a strong witness to them. Above all, remember that you are loved by a God who knows everything about you—and loves you still.

Monday
10-17

Prayer

Almighty God, it is hard to think that my identity has somehow slipped away with every passing year. Sometimes I feel forgotten when . . .

....

....

....

Help me to accept what I cannot change in others. Remind me that I am your child. My name is written on your heart. My real identity is rooted in you. Amen.

Suggestion

Turn your focus to others. Don't wait for someone to strike up a conversation. Get acquainted with a neighbor. Call an old friend. Write a letter to a grandchild. No step is too small in God's scheme of things. Whenever you feel overlooked, reread Isaiah 49:15-16.

Cards to Sadie & Cody

SUNDAY
Celebrate an acceptance of aging

Aging is part of God's plan for your life. God designed your body to change over time. You can trust God even when you don't understand the bigger divine plan. You can trust God even when you are afraid.

Give thanks for the following:

- Friends and family who can introduce you to new things and new people
- The ever-changing beauty of nature that reminds you of seasons of life
- The unique gifts that make you, you
- That you can grow stronger in faith even as your body grows weaker
- That God grieves your losses and celebrates your tenacity
- That God will never forget you. You belong to God

Write down some thoughts concerning your journey this week.

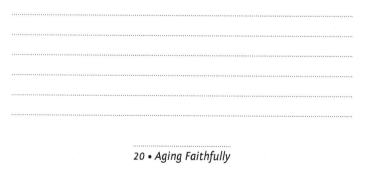

WEEK 2

Finding God's Purpose in Aging

MONDAY
Never too old

Read Romans 12:2.

For as long as you can remember, you have searched for God's will for your life. As a young person, you asked for guidance about what to study, whether to marry, what person to marry, what job to take, how to deal with a rebellious child.

Now you may feel as though you are finished seeking God's will. You have reached the pinnacle of your faith journey and have earned the right to coast through your last years. Problem is, that's not what scripture says. Nowhere is it written that we are to quit pursuing God's will in old age.

In God's kingdom, there is no resting on your spiritual laurels—no matter how old you are. No matter how frail you might become one day. God still has a plan for the rest of your life, and it is good. Think about it. Isn't it God's will that you seek God in prayer? Doesn't God want you to serve others with a humble heart? Doesn't scripture tell you always to offer God worship and praise?

Old age is no excuse for failing to be available to God. God doesn't want you to sit on the sidelines of life but to get back into the game. You can still influence others by the way you face the challenges and find the joy in aging. So don't quit living now. Your life is not over until it is over. Your story is not finished. You are never too old to be put to use by God.

Prayer

Almighty God, there are days when I think that I have put in my time. There are days when I am convinced I am too old to be useful. Yet your Word reminds me that you are the Ancient of Days who still has a purpose for my life. Today I will encourage at least three people. I name them here . . .

Julia Berryre decision on which valve surgery

Help me remember that I will never be too old for you to put me to use. Amen.

Suggestion

Study the names you wrote in the prayer above. Determine a specific action you can take today to bless and encourage each person. Give God the glory!

Thanksgiving that Julia's surgery went well & she is getting stronger. And that Ron's eye removal & valve surgery went well.

TUESDAY
Spiritually wise

Read Proverbs 1:1-7.

A man sat opposite his grandson in a booth. Throughout their lunch date, the man griped about this and that. There were too many onions on his hamburger and not enough ice in his tea. He complained about the boy's haircut before lecturing him on the perils of contemporary music. By the time the bill arrived, the boy was relieved to escape his grandfather's unpleasant ways. Despite his status as a longtime church member, the man's behavior was not very godly that afternoon. Regrettably, he had wasted an opportunity to model spiritual maturity for his younger loved one.

Let's be clear. Not every older adult is spiritually mature. Wisdom doesn't automatically come with age. It's not about how many scripture verses you can spout or the regularity of your church attendance. Spiritual maturity is the result of growing closer to Christ. Reflecting Christ's character in daily life is the fruit of spiritual maturity.

Looking back at the scene described above, it is not surprising that the grandson did not see Christ reflected in his grandfather. Thankfully you can act differently. Ask yourself a hard question: what do others see reflected in you? Do they see a judgmental nitpicker, or can they see the character of Christ?

You have much to offer the younger generations. You

have survived the school of hard knocks and have lived to tell about it. Old age brings a sweeping perspective of life that younger persons do not yet have. However, it takes a Christlike heart to share the wisdom in a way that they can hear it.

Prayer

Almighty God, I am reminded that becoming like Christ is a process of growth. I am striving to reflect his character in these ways . . .

- *kindness*
- *courage*
- *patience*

Show me how best to express the wisdom gained from my experiences in a way that draws others to you. Amen.

Suggestion

Where have you seen God's hand guiding you in the past? What positive lessons has God taught you during your long life? How can you share your wisdom so that others will want to listen?

WEDNESDAY
Servant's heart

Read John 13:13-17.

Perhaps at one time in your life you went on mission trips to repair homes. Or you stood for hours to cook for the homeless. You may have helped run an after-school program for at-risk teens. It was exhausting but exhilarating work, giving yourself to others.

Those days of physical labor are over. You just don't have the energy required any more. Besides, isn't it time for the next generation to step up to the plate and take over these tasks? Not so fast. While you may not have the energy or strength you once did, God still cares about the state of your heart. When a heart ceases to serve, it will soon grow cold and hard.

Perhaps you can't sleep on the ground in a faraway country or pound nails and carry sacks of concrete. Even so, you can serve others in a variety of ways. It is a matter of discovering those new ways.

Make yourself available to God and reflect on the possibilities. Are there missionaries or college students who would rejoice in a handwritten letter? Are there persons in the hospital or rehab center who could use a call of encouragement? Can you pray for those on the church prayer list? Could you bake a treat for a neighbor or teach a youngster a new skill?

When your heart is receptive, possibilities become endless. No task is too small or insignificant for God.

Prayer

Creator God, I want to let my late years shine for you.
Open my mind to new possibilities for serving others
right where I am. This week I will serve the following
persons ...

I have had to learn to accept
help during these past months
Rons surgeries, my Shingles, decline
since my knee surgery & fall

Let me never grow weary of serving others for you,
God. Amen.

Suggestion

Think about ways you can serve the people mentioned
in your prayer. Make a plan. Write it out. Do it.

THURSDAY
Belonging to community

Read Ephesians 4:14-16.

You were never intended to live in isolation. God did not design you to go it alone. You need the body of Christ to surround and support you. Just as importantly, the body of Christ needs you!

Certainly at times you need to retreat for renewal and meditation. Jesus understood the importance of taking time to be alone with God. But don't confuse moments of reflection and prayer with isolating yourself. God made it abundantly clear that we are to love one another and build each other up. Even the image of heaven is one of community. Yet, in aging, a tendency to withdraw may arise, especially as mobility declines. That is why it is even more crucial to stay connected to a community of believers. Don't be deceived into thinking that all you need is you.

God wants you to be in community as a way to protect you from loneliness, seclusion, and temptation. Being part of a family of faith will make you stronger than you are on your own. Remain keenly aware that too much seclusion is dangerous to your well-being.

The next time you feel inclined to isolate yourself, recall why God designed you to be a member of the body of believers. Thank God for the gift of community that encourages and strengthens you on the journey.

Prayer

Almighty God, you created us to be in community.
When I am tempted to go it alone, prompt me to . . .

Connect with others .
(Haven't been able to do this - Pandemic,
Ron's surgeries & bad health, Covid)

Help me live in the presence of others who will support
and nurture me. Amen.

Bring ribbons

Suggestion

Read Ecclesiastes 4:12. Then take three lengths
of ribbon or cording and braid them into a simple
bookmark to use in your Bible. Let this "threefold
cord" be a reminder of the need for community. If
you are not now a member of an active community of
believers, begin a study or prayer group with at least
two other persons.

FRIDAY
Embracing deep thoughts

Read Psalm 92:4-6.

One perk of growing older is having more time to think deep thoughts. During the years of raising a family or building a career, you probably enjoyed little opportunity to let your mind wander into places where you might discover profound thoughts. There was always a yard to be mowed, meals to prepare, and events to attend. Now that the pace of life has slowed, you may assume you don't have the energy to pursue thoughts that are ripe with meaning.

Think again. Now is the perfect time. Don't fear the labor of deep thinking. Just consider the vastness of your life experiences. Embrace the hard questions of life and muddle through the uncertainties. Expand your horizons. *do this*

Now is the right time to stop and look up the meaning of that word you didn't know in this morning's newspaper story. It is the time to study the constellations and to ponder migration patterns and geological wonders of the world. God gave you a magnificent mind with which to think and to shape questions. Even if your brain processes information more slowly than before, you can still think broadly and deeply. Dig in with your lifetime of experiences. Then give praise that God's ways are always higher than yours. *Stay curious*

Prayer

Almighty God, I don't consider myself a great thinker.
Yet all my life I have wondered about questions like . . .

Why am I here? Mom & Dad had Susan
then Ron. With me 5 years after Susan & 3 yrs
after Ron - 3 children in 5 years was too many

Forgive me when I am satisfied with shallow thinking
and clichéd answers. Grant me a renewed energy for
learning and a willingness to explore your thoughts.
Amen.

Suggestion

Ponder what many people consider the most important
question of all: what is the meaning of life?

Why were you born? Has your perspective about
that question changed over time? Contemplate it.
Wrestle with it. Discuss it. Then celebrate the question,
knowing that God alone has the full answer.

SATURDAY
Worship and praise

Read Romans 12:1.

At the end of a long day, an older woman turned off the TV and sat alone in the evening silence. She looked back on the day and realized that it had been a while since she had consciously thought about God. She honestly didn't remember the last time she had prayed. She couldn't even remember where she had last laid her Bible. A wave of guilt washed over her.

Maybe you can relate. You don't intend to forget God; but, in the ordinary routine of life, you do. The thing is, not a second goes by that God is not thinking of you. God has wired you for worship—not to feed God's ego but because worship opens your heart.

Of course, you have accumulated plenty of worship time over your long life: countless church services, Sunday school classes, and Bible studies. But if you think that worship is something you can store up, you are missing the point. God doesn't intend for worship to be a Sunday-only event. It is not just about singing a hymn or a halfhearted repetition of the Lord's Prayer. It's not even about hearing a great sermon.

Authentic worship is a way of life that begins anew each time you intentionally and honestly humble yourself before God. The more you acknowledge a deeper appreciation of God's power and sovereignty, the more your heart will be transformed.

Every activity you do throughout the day can be an act of worship. You can worship with a soft whisper of a prayer, thanking God for the morning light that streams through your window. You can worship by acknowledging God's creative power when you hold the tiny hands of a baby. You can worship by singing a favorite hymn while you get dressed for the day just because you want God to hear it.

Prayer

Almighty God, I thirst for communion with you. Forgive me when I fail to worship you because I become easily distracted by . . .

depression

Keep me acutely attuned to your presence throughout each day. Amen.

Suggestion

Begin a new spiritual practice. Use a notebook to write your prayers each day, even on those days when you don't feel like writing or praying. Take your time. Express praise for God's sovereignty and power. Don't be afraid to pour out your grumblings before God. Then thank God for the blessings in your life.

for us feeling your presence through this past difficult year

SUNDAY
Celebrate God's purpose in aging

It is no accident that your body ages. God designed it that way. But if you are breathing, your purpose is not over.

Give thanks for the following:

- That God has given you divine purpose until your last breath

- That God wants you to share your spiritual wisdom with others in a way they can hear it

- That God has provided ways for you to serve others even in old age

- That God designed you to live in community as a protection, for encouragement, and for strength

- That God gave you a magnificent mind and wants you to use it to think deep thoughts about God

- That God created you to offer worship and praise, not because God needs it but because worship opens your heart

Write down some thoughts concerning your journey this week. *My fatigue, pain + health*
Health Concerns — Matt + Lisa.
Ron's upcoming surgery.
Eye removal — Aug 30
Heart Valve — Nov 14

WEEK 3

Overcoming the Temptations of Aging

MONDAY
Grumbling

Read James 5:8-10.

Some people think that once you get to a certain age, you somehow have outgrown temptations. Not so. Your bent for sinning does not diminish just because you have grown older. In fact, temptations in old age are like pesky flies that just won't leave you alone.

On some days you want to grumble about every ache and pain. You feel compelled to make a snide remark and turn a cold shoulder when someone brushes past you in line. You criticize new ministry ideas at church. You even find yourself nitpicking family members about insignificant things, then wondering why they don't visit more often.

The truth is, your grumbling may be stirred up by your fear of aging. You worry that no one appreciates all that you have done in the past. You fret about what would happen if you had a stroke and had to depend on others. Or what would happen if you outlived your money? Just thinking about dreary scenarios puts you in a bad mood. Pretty soon you are taking out your foul mood on the paperboy who missed throwing the newspaper onto the front porch.

Grumbling will not get back your healthy, youthful body or the energy you once had. Habitual complaining about how much better life used to be will only make you miss out on the blessings in your life right now.

You have a choice: either let your problems stain the rest of your days, or show an attitude of gratefulness and kindness. It's up to you.

Prayer

Almighty God, save me from becoming a cranky old soul. I confess that sometimes I grumble too much about . . .

I can't think of anything I grumble about. ? Being tired ?

Inspire me to be a cheerful voice that will lift the spirits of others. Amen.

— through phone or mail
Since we have been distancing

Suggestion

Since pandemic started
TRY this starting Mon 10-24

Make a point of voicing only positive statements for the rest of this week. Catch yourself before you express a complaint. Instead, say something uplifting, even lighthearted, about the situation. Create a new habit.

TUESDAY
Clinging to your baggage

Read Matthew 11:28-30.

In some ways, aging is a process of learning to let go. You come to earth as an infant without a single possession. Years pass and you wonder how you ever accumulated so much stuff—stuff you believed you needed to be happy. Now that you have grown older, you know better. You wonder what to do with it all.

Over time you have accumulated not only material things but also emotional baggage. You have stuffed anger, rejection, and pride deep inside you like dirty clothes into laundry bags. Now that you have aged, the weight feels especially burdensome. *Bad memorys*

Jesus calls you to travel light. He wants to liberate you from both kinds of baggage that you are dragging behind you. He wants to prepare your heart to let go.

Let go of a critical spirit. Let go of things you cannot change. Let go of the resentment you harbor for someone who hurt you. Let go of self-righteous pride and the heaviness of heart that weighs you down.

Loosen your grip on material things too. You can't take that stuff with you when you leave this world. One day your loved ones will sort through the last of your belongings. The keepsakes will be passed down to future generations, but the rest will be sold or given away. God's lesson comes wrapped in a paradox. To travel light is to gain everything by letting go.

Prayer

Almighty God, I confess that I often cling to the past. Today I name these things that weigh me down and lay them at your feet . . .

God, you know what causes me such pain. Please help me to not dwell on them.

Enable me to value relationships more than objects or feelings. Give me the courage to leave my baggage behind as I travel on. Amen.

Suggestion

On a piece of paper write down those burdens you named in the prayer above. Open your Bible to Matthew 11:28-30. Reread the scripture, then place the list in your Bible, asking God to help you release your baggage. Each day for the next week reread both your list and the scripture.

Starting Monday 10-24 — one drawer, shelf, closet

MON – Thurs:

1. Today – Thanksgiving. Pantry in kitchen

Jan 2023   3 Kitchen tools drawers

WEDNESDAY
Night worries

Read Matthew 6:25-34.

Darkness finally throws its cloak over a day that you thought would never end. You can hardly wait to crawl into bed. When at last you do, you cannot sleep. You just lie awake turning over random things in your mind. Unspoken things. Troublesome issues and questions that bounce around in your imagination.

You nestle down into the covers and fluff the pillow one more time. A hard knot of worry grows in your stomach. You fidget and turn, rocking back and forth, but sleep refuses to come.

In the dark of night when there's nothing to hear but your own heartbeat, every nagging worry seems somehow worse. Little problems grow into imaginary monsters. You wrestle with them until at last you surrender, exhausted and defeated.

Worry can grow when you face many unknowns. A doctor's report. A wayward grandchild. Whether to stay in your home or move. You are tempted to worry about things great and small. But scripture repeatedly reminds you, "Fear not, I am with you."

God never intended you to go through life without a care, but God does not want you to be paralyzed by matters over which you have no control. Shift your burdens to God. Trust God. Turn your worries into prayers and let them fly heavenward.

Prayer

Almighty God, worries loom over me. I name them
now . . .

Our children, my bodily indignities as I get older, my health & my family's health

Help me to trust you even when I am afraid. Amen.

Suggestion

Begin the day by saying aloud, "God, you are bigger
than *my worries* ." Fill in the blank with each
worry you listed above. Before you go to bed at night,
repeat the activity.

I have not taken care of my health, especially this year. Help me to get my diet (diabetic) under control. Help me to not feel unworthy if I don't do as much as I think I should. Help me to find joy in the following, not guilt:

— art & painting
— reading
— sewing
— physical activity as much as I'm able & no regret if I can't

THURSDAY
Giving up on life

Let us not become weary in doing good For at the proper time we will reap a harvest if we do not give up 10 Therefore as we have opportunity let us do good to all people especially those who belong to the family of believers

Read Galatians 6:9-10.

A woman crawled out of bed to close the window blinds. She really wanted to close out the world. When she got back in bed and pulled the covers over her head, she wished that death would take her soon. Her best friend and husband of almost sixty years had died recently. She had never felt more lonely than she did at that moment.

You may be tempted to give up on life too. The challenges of this season can be exhausting at times, leaving you broken and depleted. Or perhaps you struggle with too much dull routine. You wonder if you have purpose on this earth.

It's not uncommon for older adults to become depressed. Often physical reasons account for depression; these require medical attention and can be treated with medication. Other times, combating depression becomes a matter of guarding your mind against bleak thoughts.

In the scripture passage, Paul reminds his readers not to become weary in doing good and not to give up. God wants you to keep ministering to others, even when what you are doing seems so insignificant. God is there in every challenge you are facing. God wants to strengthen your spiritual core and empower you to move on. One day at a time, one step at a time.

Prayer

Patient God, keep me from being a person who chooses to quit living. I have been overwhelmed with depressing feelings about . . , *the health of all of my family, growing older & not being able to do as much. The personal indignities of growing older.*

Give me the wisdom to seek medical attention for depression when needed. Help me also to resist dark thoughts that invade my mind. Amen.

Suggestion

Ask a friend to become your "blessing buddy." Take turns calling each other every day and share three blessings you have discovered that day.

Oct 26, 2022,
1. Got out of the house & we went to Walmart
2. Matt is feeling better.
3. Groceries to day & put away.

Oct 30, SAt
1. Call from my friend, Sandy Brady.
2. Watching old episodes of The Waltons,
3. Text from friend Jane Loomis,
1-26-23 that I was able to shovel a path through 6" of snow, house to mailbox

FRIDAY
Getting lost in the messiness

Read Jeremiah 29:11-13.

Looking back on life can be bittersweet. Along with heartwarming memories of family and friends, there are experiences you would rather forget. Times when life mowed you down and spit you out as a shredded mess. Sometimes your mind insists on wandering back through life's crooked paths.

How you wish you could undo those hurtful moments. But even if you could, what about the good that may have come out of those bad times? What about the insights gained from painful experience?

One thing is clear. Life is messy. It hasn't always turned out the way you had planned. Heartaches and disappointments were real: difficult family members, financial worries, health issues, career regrets. But there have been many good times and treasured memories.

You have come to appreciate life's ups and downs as part of your own unique adventure. No one else has experienced your journey. And throughout it all, God has never left you. Not once. Not even when you thought God was nowhere around.

You never have to wait until your life is tidy and neat before you come to God. God already knows your messiness—and loves you still. In fact, God delights in using imperfect people just like you to do good work in the world—even now at this late stage.

To live is to know both the joys and the sorrows of life. Go ahead. Pour out your messiness before a God who adores you just as you are. You can trust God to perfect the sojourner who continues on this spiritual pilgrimage that is life.

Prayer

Loving God, I confess that I have not been able to comprehend what you are doing in my life right now. Yet when I look back, I can see that your hand has guided me through messy times of life like when . . .

This past year, 2022, Judy Knee Surgery, blood clot, kidney stone worsening scoliosis. Ron melanoma progressively worse, loss of his eye, aortic valve replacement & recovery, both isolation to prevent

Thank you for loving me just as I am. Amen. *Covid & other*

Suggestion

16-24-22

Spend time focusing on the blessings that God brought out of each of the messes you listed above.

Help & love from family & friends, good doctors, Our relationship with each other.

Read Proverbs 15. Do

A retired man gritted his teeth until his jaw began to ache from being clenched so hard. Just thinking about how someone had wronged him years ago triggered an inner rage he considered buried. He wondered how he could still be so angry after all this time.

In this season of life, you have more time to think about the past. You glance back at your life and see those times when your bitterness erupted all over innocent people. Now you realize that your unwillingness to forgive even contaminated your relationship with God.

You don't mean to be bitter, but the idea of forgiving someone who hurt you seems almost unbearable. Here's the thing: forgiveness doesn't change the wrong that was done, but bitterness will change you from the person God wants you to be. Think about it. With God, hearts can be transformed. It's not too late.

Prayer

Merciful God, I pray that you would faithfully change my heart. I confess that I have not forgiven . . . *the hurtful things that were done and the words that were said to deliberitly hurt me. How can I not feel bitter*

Please turn my bitterness into forgiveness and help me move on. Amen.

Suggestion

Think about what you can do this week to keep from becoming bitter as you age. How might you be letting your fear or anger control your thoughts? Who else do you need to forgive?

SUNDAY
Celebrate victory over temptations

Give thanks for the following:

- That God enables you to overcome negative thoughts and comments by helping you develop a new attitude of gratitude and service
- That God is willing to carry your burdens—including your emotional baggage
- That God is bigger than any worry you may have
- That God will refresh you and guide you in finding new enthusiasm for living
- That God has brought you through failures and hard times in this great adventure of life
- That God can turn your bitterness to forgiveness

....

....

....

....

Write down some thoughts concerning your journey this week.

....

....

....

....

....

WEEK 4

....

Discovering the Joys of Aging

MONDAY
Preaching your own eulogy

Read 2 Timothy 4:6-8.

To preach your own eulogy seems an odd thing, an impossible thing. On the other hand, it makes perfect sense. What better way to give a funeral sermon than to live well until the very end? It's not really a morbid thought. It is a unique opportunity.

Now is the time to consider how to complete your life story in a way that will leave a significant imprint on the hearts and minds of others. You have the chance to teach important life lessons that are best demonstrated by one who has lived through many seasons. You can model perseverance and courage, demonstrating that a bend in the road of life is not the end of the journey. You can show others how to value their own lives and not waste time trying to live someone else's life.

With each new day, you can still shape the way people will remember you long after you are gone. Will you show them an irresistible positive attitude about life? Will you show them how to seize each moment with a grateful heart? Will you live so that they recognize faith in the face of death?

The final chapters of your life are not so much about what you have done in the past but about how you are living in the now. What difference are you making today? Don't be a "cold saint," a faithful servant who has grown cold with age. You can say no to becoming a person who quits living long before death arrives. You can be in ministry even in retirement. You can be the faithful disciple who continues to find joy in the winter of life so that God's glory can be seen. Now is your chance to be the best funeral sermon you can.

Prayer

Almighty God, I pray that you will give me the strength and courage to faithfully live out the rest of my life. Forgive me for the times that I have been a cold saint, times I . . .

....

....

....

Inspire me to live fully until my last breath. Amen.

Suggestion

Think of someone outside your family on whom you might make a positive impact. What can you do this week to initiate or continue your good influence?

TUESDAY
Answered prayer

Read Psalm 5:2-3.

At times you may have treated God like a bubblegum machine. You dropped a coin in the prayer slot and expected an answered prayer to roll out. But perhaps the answers that tumbled out were not always what you expected. In fact, God hasn't always acted the way you thought God would or should.

At other times you wondered if God was listening at all. Silence left you thinking God had abandoned you. Sometimes you even prayed as if it was up to you to tell God what to do. Now that you have grown older, there are days when words for prayer just won't come. You struggle to string thoughts together in a way that makes sense. But deep down inside, something stirs your soul and prompts you to keep praying.

Over the years, you have prayed for wisdom and guidance, for good health and godly children. Even after all the prayers you have said, prayer remains mysterious. Now, though, you have the advantage of looking back over life to reflect on how God responded to your prayers, how God brought good out of bad situations. From this vantage point you can finally make sense of much that didn't make sense before. Growing older allows you to shift your perspective toward God's way of seeing things.

Prayer and aging go hand in hand. An active prayer

life provides you a constant source of friendship. Nothing is too insignificant or too overwhelming to tell your heavenly Father. Walk closely with God and feel divine goodness all around you.

Prayer

Gracious God, I thank you for the answered prayers in my life, especially . . .

Ron's successful surgeries

Quiet the noises in my soul and let me hear you. Be near to me in this journey. Amen.

Suggestion

Pray for family—brothers, sisters, children, grandchildren, great-grandchildren, others—and for friends by name. Pray that you will discover something new today. Pray for someone who is having a difficult season of life. Pray that your life will touch a stranger who doesn't know how much he or she needs God.

WEDNESDAY
Something to laugh about

Read Psalm 126:2.

Four women gather around the same table in a local café each Tuesday at noon. You can always recognize them by the infectious laughter that bounces off the walls whenever they are together.

Don't think for a moment that life has been all fun and games for this group of friends. Their recent years have been filled with heartache and loss. Two of the women are newly widowed. Another continues her twelve-year battle with cancer. The fourth has macular degeneration and depends on the others to assist her in almost every task. Even so, this group of friends believes strongly in the healing power of laughter, especially as they have aged.

You too have discovered the importance of using humor to get through tough times. It is far easier to laugh about a mind that limps along like a three-legged dog than it is to fret over every lapse in memory.

Shared laughter is a gift, a holy antidote to the challenges of aging. It connects you to others and allows you to deal with burdens in a positive way. Not surprisingly, people enjoy being around other people who laugh.

Perhaps God created humor as a way to decrease stress and build community. When fear and discouragement pound at your door, laughter is the best way to answer it. Go ahead now. Feeling tension and worry? Lighten up! Find something funny in the moment. Keep laughing until your last breath.

Prayer

Almighty God, help me harness the power of laughter in my life. Show me how to find the humor in difficult situations like . . .

....

....

....

Thank you for the gift of holy laughter. Amen.

Suggestion

Be intentional in your effort to laugh. Sometime during the next week, share a joke, cartoon, or funny story with others. When something happens to cause you worry, look for what may be funny in the circumstances.

THURSDAY
Right on time

Read Psalm 39:4-5.

God's timetable is impossible to comprehend. Try as you might, you cannot see time as God sees it. In fact, it's hard to imagine that your long life represents but a breath in the span of eternity.

In many ways, time conjures up a strange push-pull of emotions. When you look back across the years, it seems that time has zipped by. You have celebrated more than sixty, seventy, eighty, or ninety birthdays in your lifetime. Yet except for a few milestone celebrations, you can't distinguish one birthday from another. On the other hand, you remember being a youngster who thought the next birthday would never come.

Throughout your days, you have experienced moments so unbelievably good you wished you could have saved them in a bottle. Special vacations. Family holidays. Graduations. A grandchild's wedding. But dark days scarred by death, loss, and rejection also mark the past. Nestled between the joys and the sorrows, countless ordinary days slipped by with little notice. Now that you have reached the golden years, it seems odd to think that the days have each held the same number of hours, yet they have felt so different.

Sometimes the hours of your day drone on endlessly. You begin to wonder whether God has made a mistake in numbering your days. The answer is no. God's timing is perfect. God has a plan for your life. And God's eternal time line won't stop with the last step of your earthly journey.

Prayer

Infinite God, time is both precarious and precious. I realize that I often spend too much time . . .

....

and not enough time . . .

....

Help me remember that your timing is perfect. Amen.

Suggestion

Write a prescription for using your time well today. Determine what is most important and how you will include these elements in your day.

FRIDAY
Saving the best for last

Read Philippians 3:12-14.

You have heard people talk about saving the best for last. In this season of life, that expression can seem more like a cruel joke. How can dealing with aching joints and diminished eyesight be the best of times? Even so, with the finish line on the distant horizon, you can glance back and see that your race has been full of adventure. You have survived unexpected twists and turns and dramatic ups and downs. At this stage of the race, a deep sense of peace and contentment sweeps over you. A sense of quiet joy wells up.

Over the years, the pressure to keep up with the Joneses has dissipated. You are finally comfortable in your own skin, even if it is a little wrinkled. The kids are reared, and your career is likely a thing of the past. It seems you can now concentrate energy fully on what is most important in life: relationships. Relationships with family and friends. Relationship with God.

It is true that even as you grow physically weaker, you can grow spiritually stronger. With every trial, you learn to trust God's character and promises more. That is God's way. You have reached a point in life when you realize that God is the only strength you have left. No antiaging product can save you. No medical procedure will turn back the clock. No bank account can give you eternity.

Only when you fully embrace your mortality can you really live, authentically and unafraid. The finish line is getting closer with each day, but you have unshakable confidence that the best is yet to be.

Prayer

Almighty God, you have created life to be a journey. Until you call me home, enable me to live faithfully and obediently. I celebrate loved ones who have finished the race before me and call them by name . . . *Susan, Ron, Beth, Doris, Mom & Dad, Anna Jane, Cora Ethel, Alice, Pat Dalton*

Keep my eyes focused on you until at last I cross the finish line and hear the joy of heaven breaking forth. Amen.

Suggestion

Think of a joyous family reunion or a celebration that you experienced in the past. Remember the warm embraces and the laughter. Now imagine the loved ones you listed above standing alongside, cheering you on to a victorious finish.

SATURDAY
Leaving a legacy

Read Psalm 71:17-18.

It has been said that what you do for yourself will die when you die, but what you have done for others will live on forever. Like a gardener who lovingly tends flowering bulbs and trees so that others, even strangers, can enjoy them long after she is gone, an individual can leave a beautiful legacy.

In God's way of thinking, legacy is about other people. It is not measured in money or valuable objects but in selfless acts of love. After you die, no one will really care about whether or not you drove a luxury car or a dented old pickup. They will not be inspired to be better people by your diamond ring or collection of gold coins. What they will remember most is how well you loved them.

Think for a moment about people who have made your life richer by the way they lived theirs. Probably many have been gone for years, yet their influence continues. Which ones taught you about God? Who shared life stories that encouraged you when the world was caving in around you? Who made you feel special when others said you were worthless?

The legacy you are creating with each new day was shaped in part by these people. They blessed you in a way that has extended to this very moment and will extend into the future by way of your own legacy.

The bottom line is simple. You already know how the story will end. Your mortal body will wear out one day. What will remain is the impact you have made upon the lives of others. You cannot fully grasp its reaches. You have no idea of the fullness of your influence.

Prayer

Almighty God, I long to be remembered as a person who . . .

....

....

....

Especially now, help me live so others can see the reflection of Christ in me. Amen.

Suggestion

Walk through your home and look at photographs. Whisper a word of thanks for the people in each photo. Then as you go through your day, be intentional about greeting and smiling at each person you pass.

SUNDAY
Celebrate the blessings

Give thanks for the following:

- That you have the opportunity to influence others with how you are living today
- That you can look back over a long life and see how God has answered your prayers
- That God gave you the gift of laughter and humor to soften the sharp edges of growing old
- That God's time is perfect even when you don't understand it
- That you can grow stronger in faith even as you grow weaker physically
- That your life will continue to shape others long after you are gone

....

....

....

....

Write down some thoughts concerning your journey this week.

....

....

....

....

REFLECTION QUESTIONS

The following questions are designed for small-group discussions or to stimulate deeper thought by individuals on each of the four topics. Complete each week's readings, prayers, and activities before reflecting on these questions.

Week 1: Accepting the Challenges of Aging

1. Describe a recent time when you felt out of step with the world. How did you react to the situation? Does reflecting on the timeless characteristics of Christ help shift your negative feelings?

2. In what ways do people try to deny the hard truths of aging? How can you balance the hard truths with God's good purpose in aging? What effect has aging had on your passion for living?

3. Mark Twain said, "Age is an issue of mind over matter. If you don't mind, it doesn't matter." In what ways does that ring true for you? In what ways does it not?

4. What troubles you most about growing physically weaker as you age? Describe a recent occasion when your physical strength was not enough to fulfill a task. How did that situation make you feel? What exercises can you do to strengthen your physical body? What about strengthening your faith?

5. Loss and aging are companions in life. No one reaches old age without grieving many significant losses. For what or for whom are you grieving in this season of life? Do you feel God's presence in your mourning? How might you seek God today?

6. As you age, it is easy to lose a sense of identity. Think of a time when you felt overlooked or rejected. Now ponder your spiritual identity. Reflect on Psalm 139:4; 1 Corinthians 15:10; and Ephesians 2:10.

7. In what ways has our culture warped God's view of aging?

Week 2: Finding God's Purpose in Aging

1. How do you understand God's purpose for your life? Why were you created? What has shaped your understanding of God? As you continue to age, how are you pursuing a purpose bigger than yourself?

2. How would you describe the difference between human wisdom and God's wisdom? Why is

wisdom particularly important as you grow older? At this stage of life, how can you continue to grow in wisdom? If godly wisdom is best expressed through relationship, how might you change the way you give counsel so that younger people will want to hear what you have to say?

3. Do you sometimes dwell on what you cannot do because of mobility or health issues? Make a list of ten things you can do in spite of your limitations.

4. Think about times when you isolated yourself for a long period. How did the isolation affect you? Think about times when you have felt the nurturing spirit of a faith community. Write down or share with others some ways that you can build a stronger sense of community in your current circumstance.

5. Read Isaiah 55:8-9. How does fixing your mind on God's thoughts as you age strengthen you?

6. As people age, their church attendance may become irregular because of physical decline. How can you continue to be a part of corporate worship, even as you are growing older? People sometimes confuse authentic worship with church attendance. Reflect on Psalm 146: how do you express praise and worship?

7. The purposeful life is not always a comfortable life. In what ways have you experienced the truth that hard times are most often temporary? How do you see life's challenges as a part of your faith journey?

Week 3: Overcoming the Temptations of Aging

1. An aging person may tend to blame society's woes on others, especially younger generations. In what ways might that be unfair? When you are tempted to feel sorry for yourself or to be prideful, how does Colossians 3:12 suggest you respond? What can you do to keep from being grumpy or critical when the temptation is strong?

2. How might you be clinging to the past in ways that are unhealthy and unwise? How can you celebrate the past without becoming entangled by it?

3. It is easy to fill your mind with "what ifs" of worst-case scenarios. What does Philippians 4:8 say about that? What do you take away from Psalm 94:19 on the subject of worrying?

4. Is giving up on life ever an option for a Christian? Reflect on the difference between giving up and a godly acceptance of one's circumstances.

5. Some say that life is what happens while you are waiting for all the puzzle pieces to fit perfectly together. Do you agree or not? Explain.

6. Sometimes people swap fear for bitterness. It can seem easier to be bitter about circumstances out of your control than to deal with issues of insecurity or forgiveness. Are you afraid to forgive someone for a past hurt? Think of a time

in your life when you let unforgiveness seep into your life. Read Hebrews 12:15 and discuss.

7. After the prophet Elijah experienced deep despair and isolation, God came to Elijah, not in the wind, earthquake, or fire but in a quiet whisper. Read 1 Kings 19 to get a perspective on Elijah's depression and how God showed him there was still a divine plan for his life.

Week 4: Discovering the Joys of Aging

1. Many people avoid the topic of growing old, yet God created aging. God designed the human body to change over time. How does having a Christian perspective enable you to embrace aging as a gift?

2. Look back at your life. Can you think of a time when God trumped the answer you wanted to a prayer with an answer that was beyond anything you had ever imagined? Think of times when you had to wait on God's answer. What was the outcome? Do you have prayers that still go unanswered? Prayer trains your eyes on the heart of God. It is the best defense you have against the negative perceptions of aging. Write a prayer asking God to help you deepen your prayer life.

3. Describe a time when laughter spontaneously spilled over and changed a situation. When was the last time a dose of humor helped you cope with a difficult situation?

4. When you gaze at life in the rearview mirror, what is your perspective on time? Over the years, how has your perspective on time shifted? Do you see time as an enemy or a friend? Explain your answer. In what practical ways could you try to see time as God sees time.

5. How has your long life already brought you unexpected joy? Where do you expect to find joy in the future?

6. Some people feel as though their best times are behind them, but as a Christian you are called to lean forward into life. In what ways can you embrace the fullness of your years in your current circumstances?

7. In what ways can you better focus on what will outlive you? How can you invest your earthly time and energy into eternity?

DEDICATION

I dedicate this book to
Mrs. Lucimarian Roberts,
a woman of great faith
who is teaching others how to age gracefully.

ACKNOWLEDGMENTS

I am so grateful for the many older adults in my life who have made their lives both transparent and accessible to me, most especially, for John Quinlan, whose friendship and wisdom have been immeasurable.

I want to acknowledge Janice Neely and Jill Ridenour, the dynamic marketing duo at Upper Room Books whose tireless energy and ideas inspire me daily. Thanks also to Robin Pippin, editorial director at Upper Room Books, who has so graciously supported my passion and ministry to, for, and with older adults.

Finally, thanks to my family. To my children and their spouses who have grown into the most remarkable adults. To my grandchildren, who let me play on the floor with them. And to my husband, Barry, for loving me unconditionally and walking beside me on this great journey of life.

ABOUT THE AUTHOR

MISSY BUCHANAN is an author, columnist, radio show host, blogger, and speaker on issues of aging and faith. She is the author of several top-selling books for Upper Room Books: *Don't Write My Obituary Just Yet*, *Talking with God in Old Age*, and *Living with Purpose in a Worn-Out Body*.

Missy also writes a monthly column, "Aging Well," for *The United Methodist Reporter* and has written feature articles for many publications including, *Presbyterians Today*, *Mature Years*, and *Response*. She hosts *Aging and Faith with Missy Buchanan* on Blog Talk Radio.

Find out more about Missy at
www.missybuchanan.com.
Follow her on Twitter
@MissyBuchanan

MORE BOOKS BY MISSY BUCHANAN

DON'T WRITE MY OBITUARY JUST YET
ISBN 978-0-8358-1046-3

**TALKING WITH GOD IN OLD AGE:
MEDITATIONS AND PSALMS**
ISBN 978-0-8358-1016-6

LIVING WITH PURPOSE IN A WORN-OUT BODY
ISBN 978-0-8358-9942-0

* * * * *

MORE 28-DAYS-OF-PRAYER BOOKS

FACING FINANCIAL STRUGGLE
by Wessel Bentley
ISBN 978-0-8358-1027-2

PRAYING THROUGH A CHILD'S ILLNESS
by Wessel Bentley
ISBN 978-0-8358-1064-7

**Order online at
bookstore.upperroom.org
or call
1-800-972-0433**

Sunday Mass
10 AM   Channel 33

CPSIA information can be obtained
at www.ICGtesting.com
Printed in the USA
BVHW070020250919
559331BV00005B/8/P

9 780835 810630